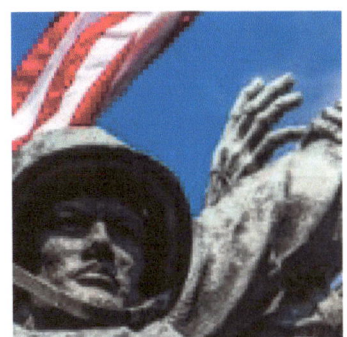 # The Brave, The Courageous

To:

From:

Copyright © 2021

All Rights Reserved.

No part of this publication may be reproduced, distributed, or transmitted in any form or by any means, including photocopying, recording, or other electronic or mechanical methods, without the prior written permission of the author.

From the bitter cold winter at Valley Forge, to the mountains of Afghanistan and the deserts of Iraq, our soldiers have courageously answered when called, gone where ordered, and defended our nation with honor.

≈ Solomon Ortiz

This is a war to end all wars.

~ Woodrow Wilson

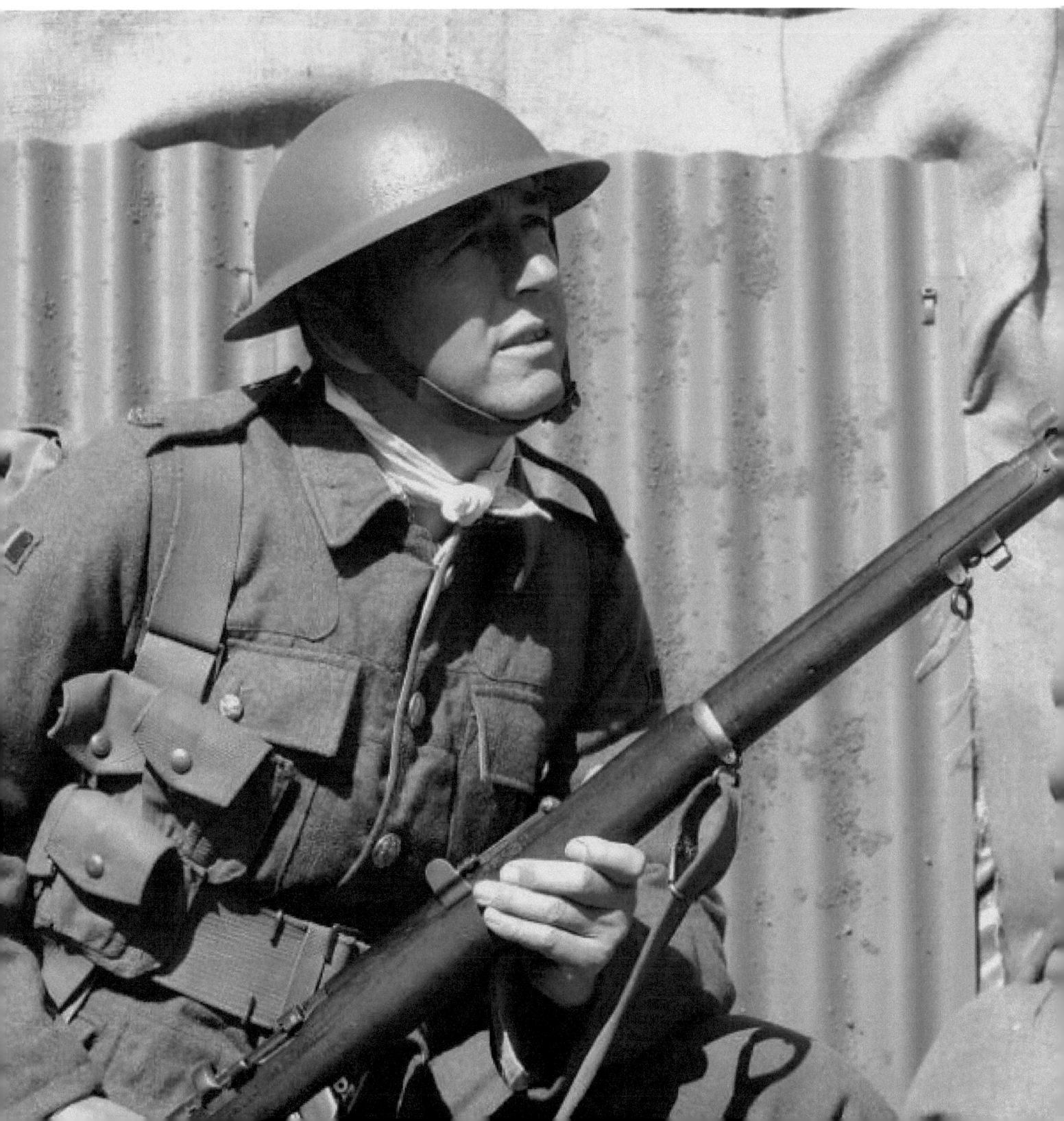

The First World War was a horror of gas, industrialized slaughter fear and appalling human suffering.

~ Nick Harkaway

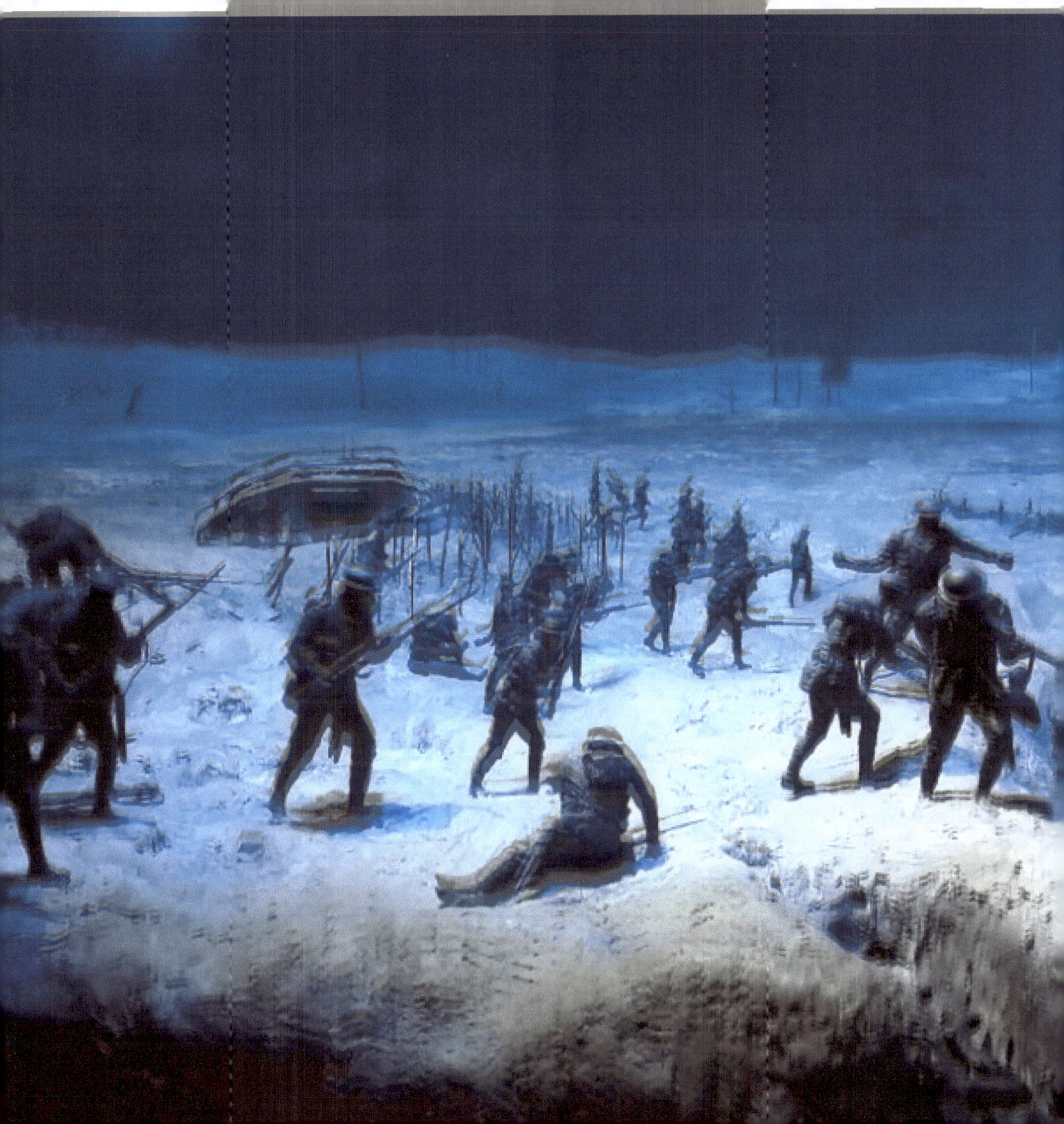

I wish those people who talk about going on with this war whatever it costs could see the soldiers suffering from mustard gas poisoning. Great mustard-coloured blisters, blind eyes, all sticky and stuck together, always fighting for breath, with voices a mere whisper, saying that their throats are closing and they know they will choke.

~ Nurse Vera Brittain

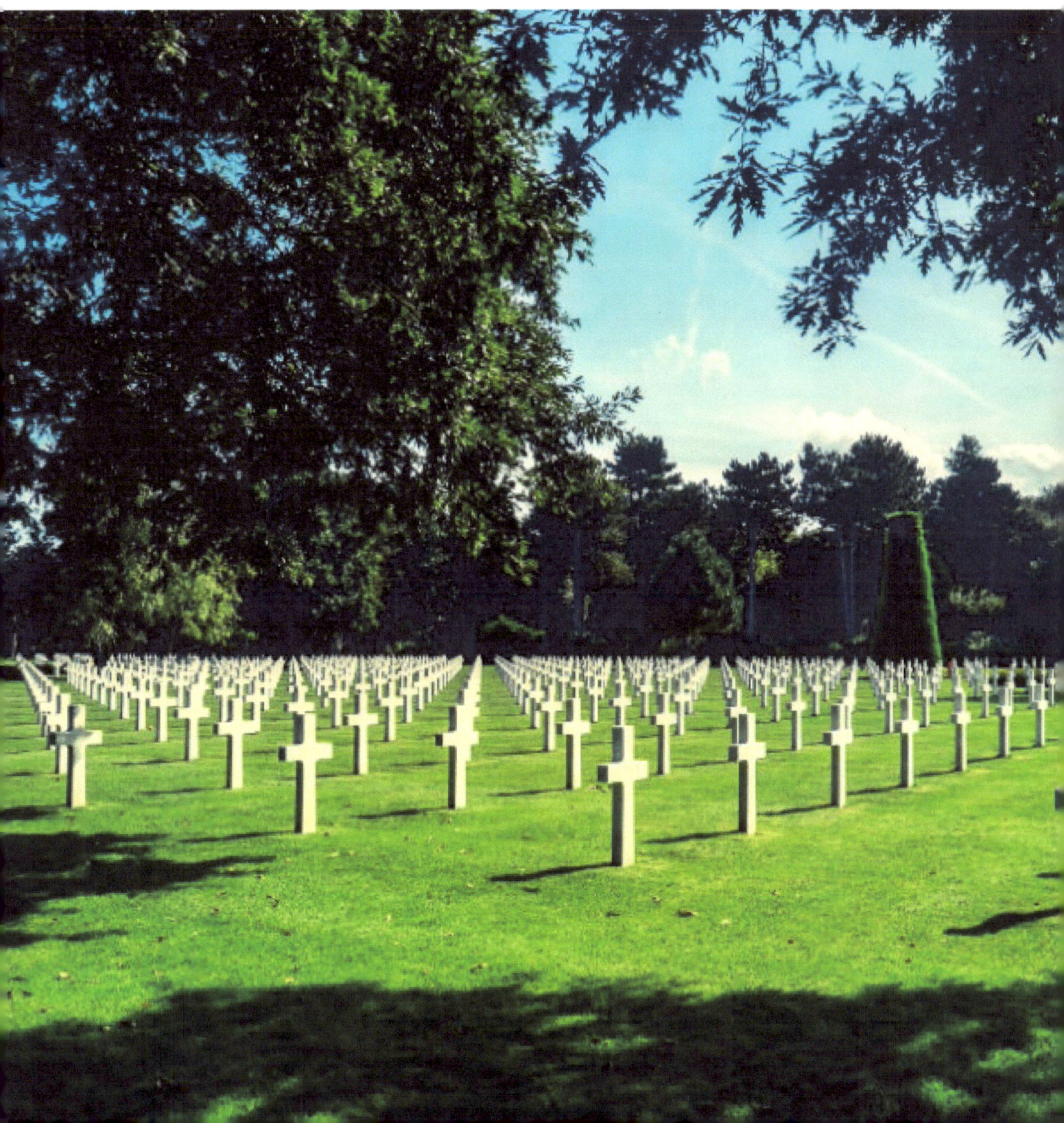

My Father was a veteran of World War II. He carried a bazooka at the Battle Of The Bulge. He wanted so much to see the WWII Memorial in Washington, D.C. I made sure that happened. My Dad walked with a cane but we saw every inch of the Memorial.

As we were sitting on a bench outside the memorial, a biker stopped and asked my Dad if he had served in WWII. When my Dad responded he had, the biker responded with "Thank you for your service". I'm not sure I've ever seen a bigger smile on my Dad's face.

≈ B. T. Robb

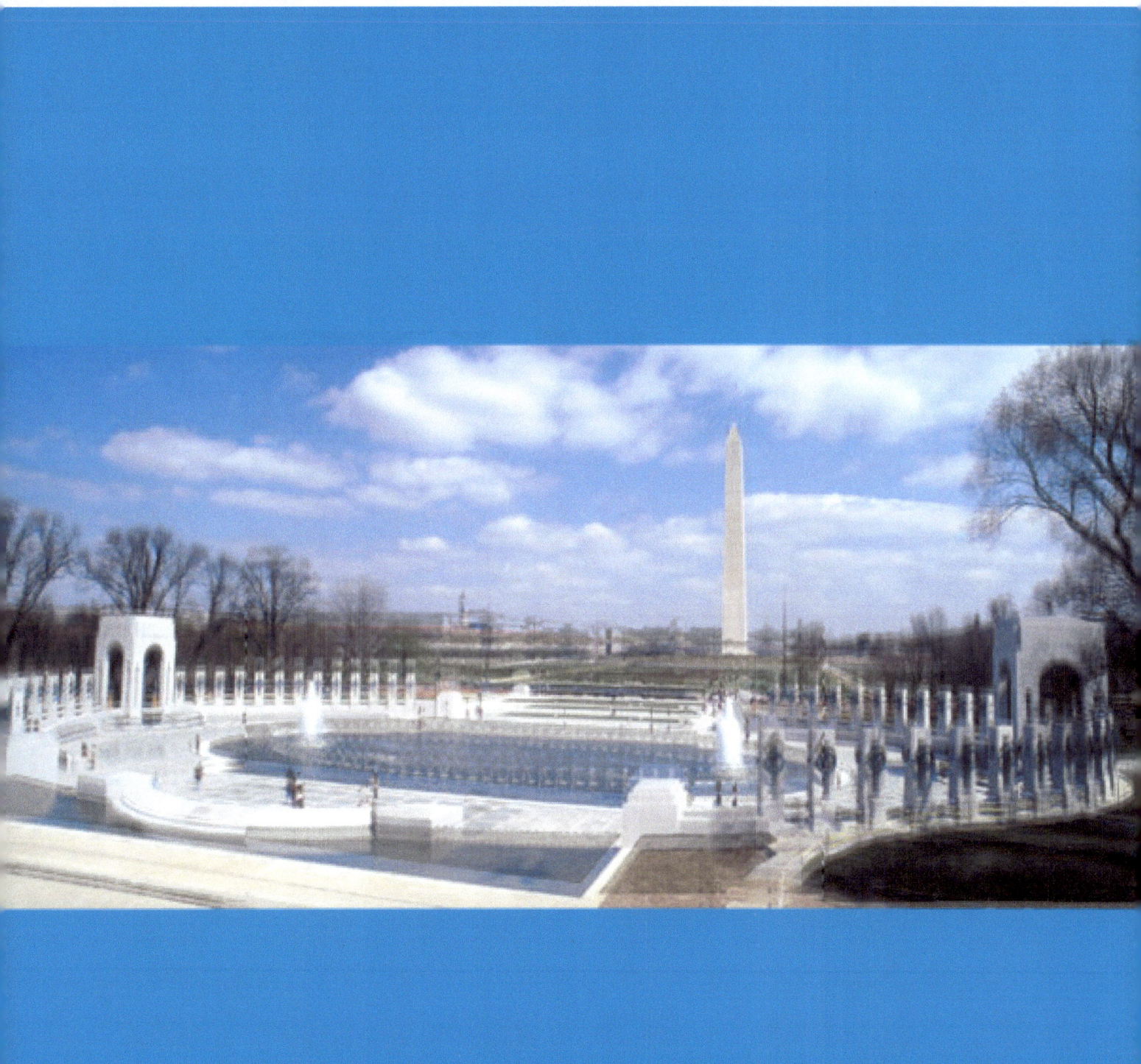

Heroic U.S. Marines raising the flag of the country they love and are fighting for to keep us free while experiencing the loss of many of their comrades.

~ B. T. Robb

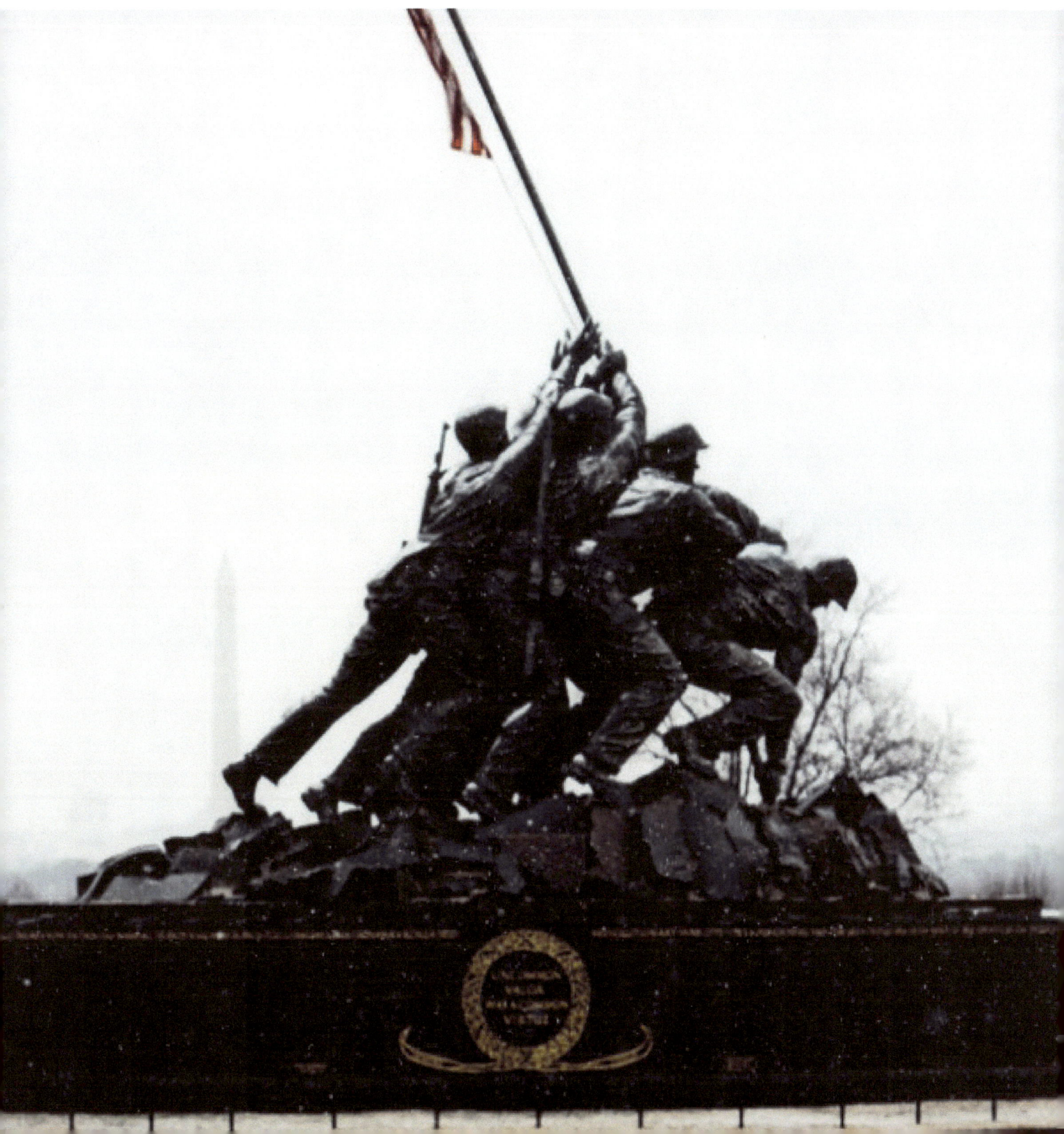

There is no substitute for victory.

~ General Douglas MacArthur

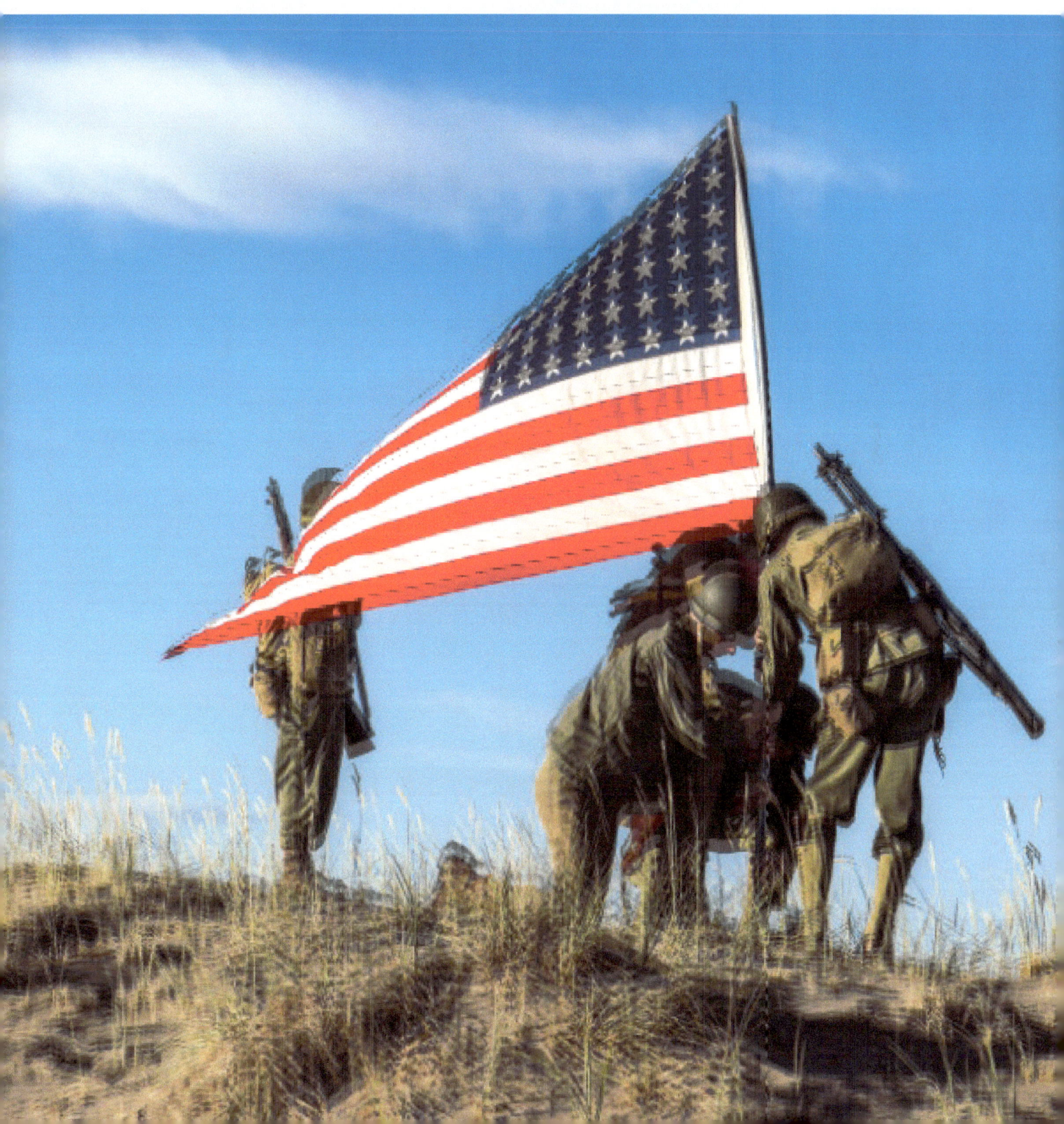

Our soldiers fought in the Korean War to push back communism. As a result of their effort and the effort of our allies, South Korea is free today.

~ Pierre Poilievre

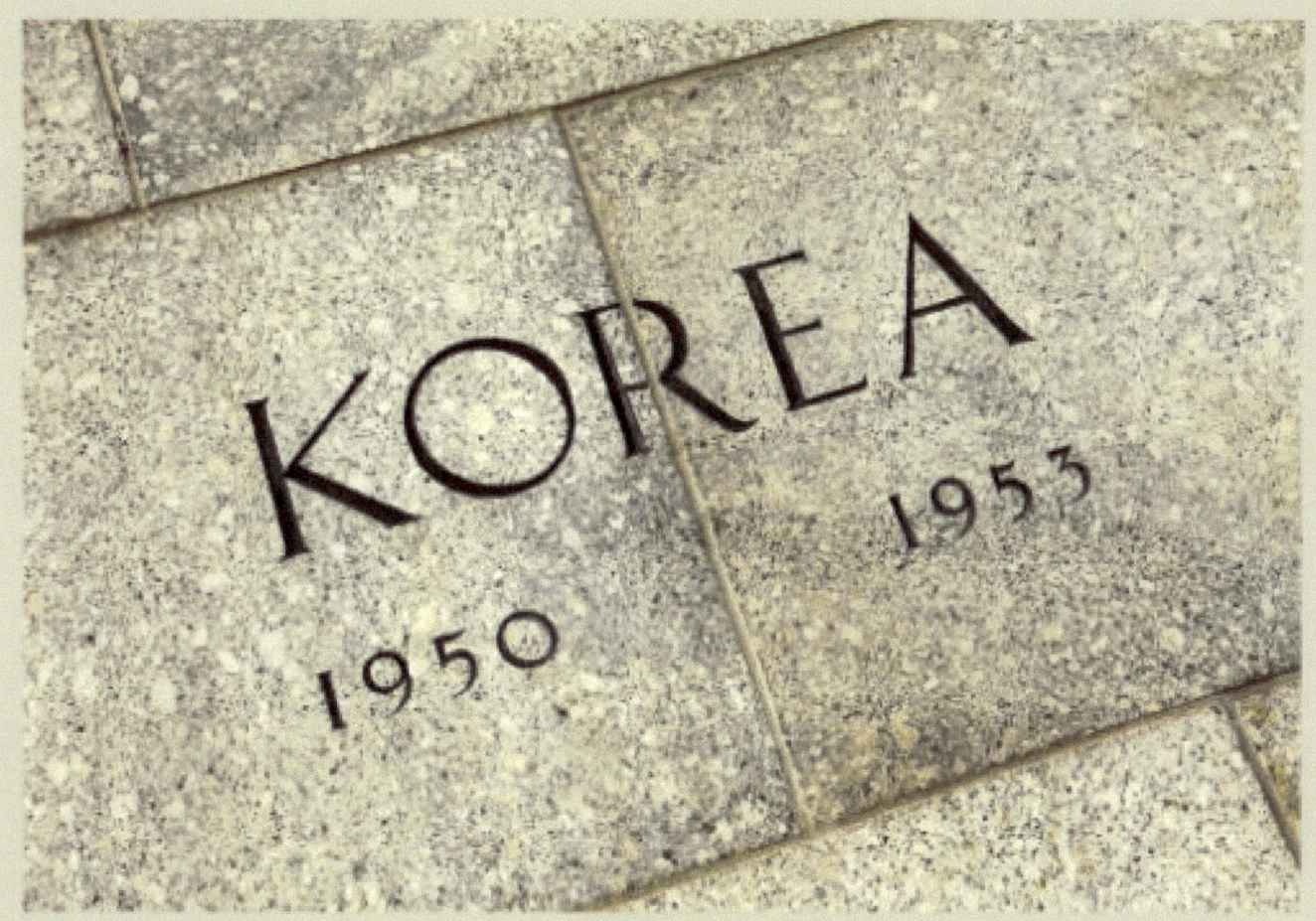

In my generation, this was not the first occasion when the strong had attacked the weak. Communism was acting in Korea just as Hitler, Mussolini, and the Japanese had acted ten, fifteen, and twenty years earlier. I felt certain that if South Korea was allowed to fall, communist leaders would be emboldened to override nations closer to our own shores."

~ President Harry Truman

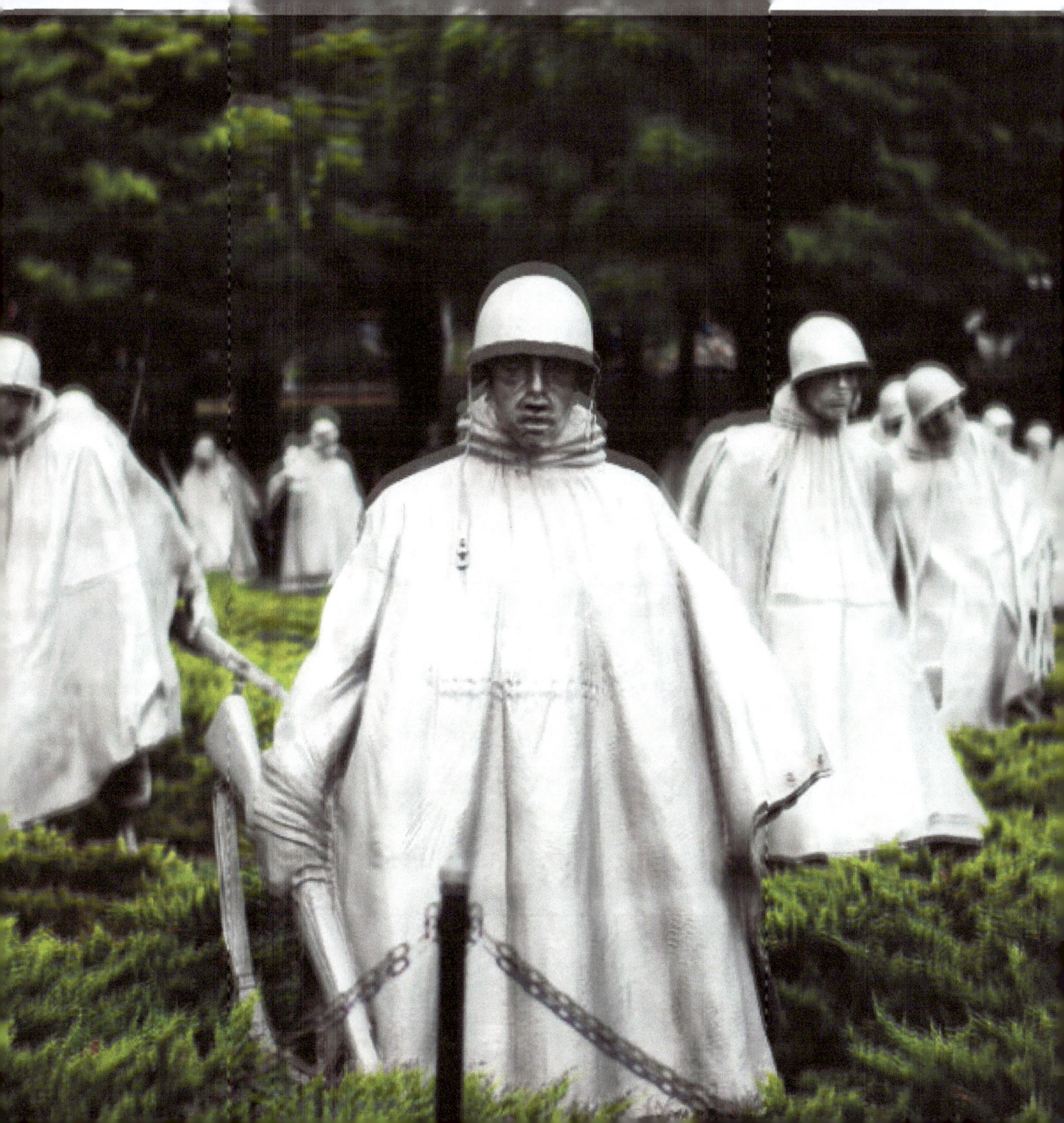

As a Korean War Veteran, I know too well the troubling nature of war. This is why I will always support a diplomatic answer before military intervention.

~ Charles B. Rangel

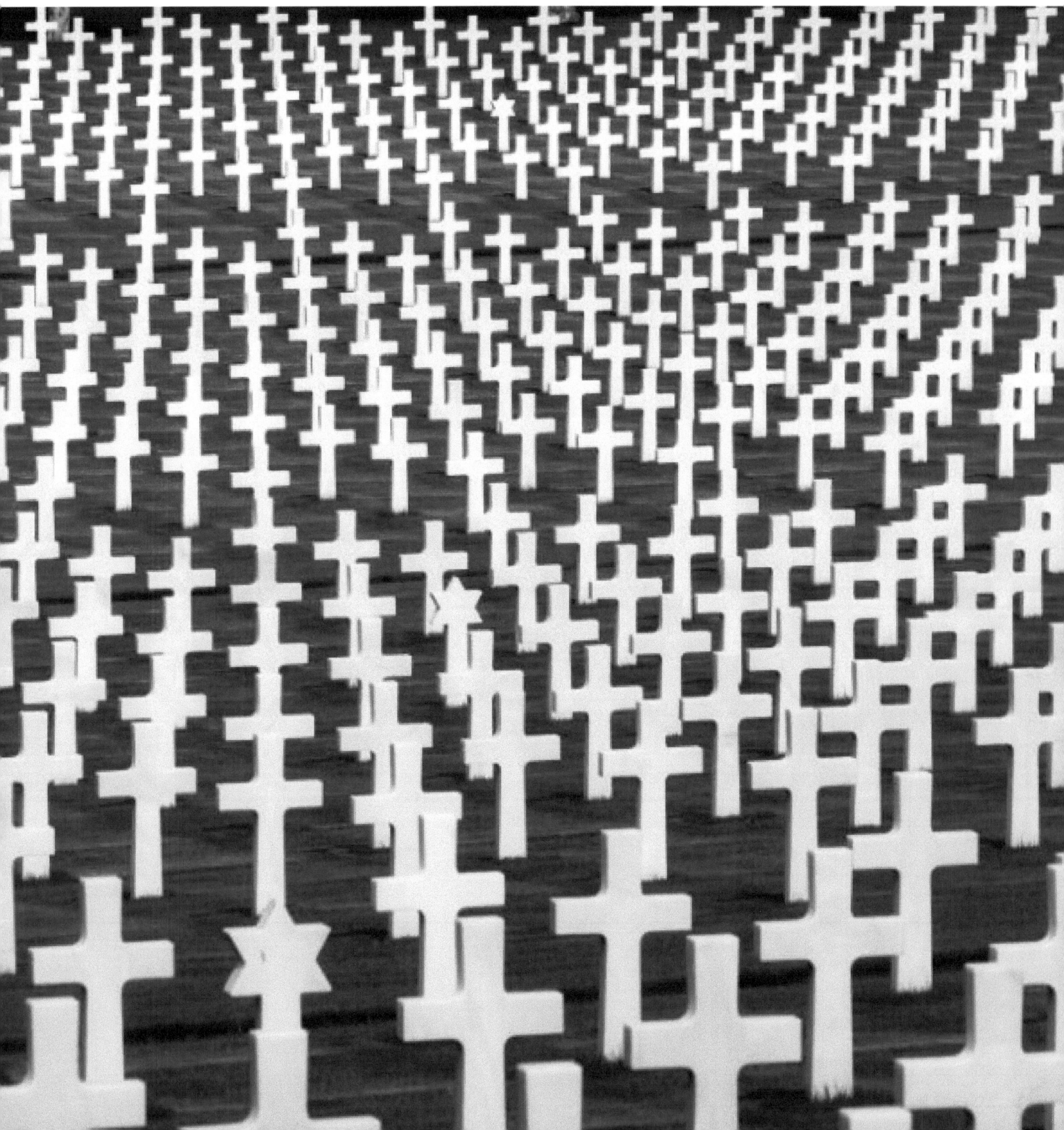

This is the war that many still call a "police action" rather than a war. Try to tell the families of the 10's of thousands of lives that were lost or those that were there. Including myself.

≈ B. T. Robb

VIETNAM
1962 — 1973
1975

There are currently 58,320 names on the Vietnam Memorial as of 2018. However, the official number of U.S Vietnam deaths was reported to be 58,220 in May, 2018. May God rest their courageous souls

~ B. T. Robb

... JOHN ELLISON
JOHN R HILL · HARLAN E HAHN
...IAM J LEVETT · MICHAEL N HUBERT
JAMES NICKENS · HAROLD S LEWIS
ROYSTON · JOHN C ODLE
... D R SIMMERS · RICHARD W FORD
... C JOYCE · GARY W SMITH
... · ARTHUR W BARTLETT Sr · JOSEPH A WEBER
... HOGAN · RICHARD C BRUNN
...DRENO · FRANCIS W CODY
... G DALEY · KENNETH DAVIS
... DOUGLAS B FORSBERG

How do you ask a man to be the last man to die in Vietnam? How do you ask a man to be the last man to die for a mistake?

≈ John F. Kerry

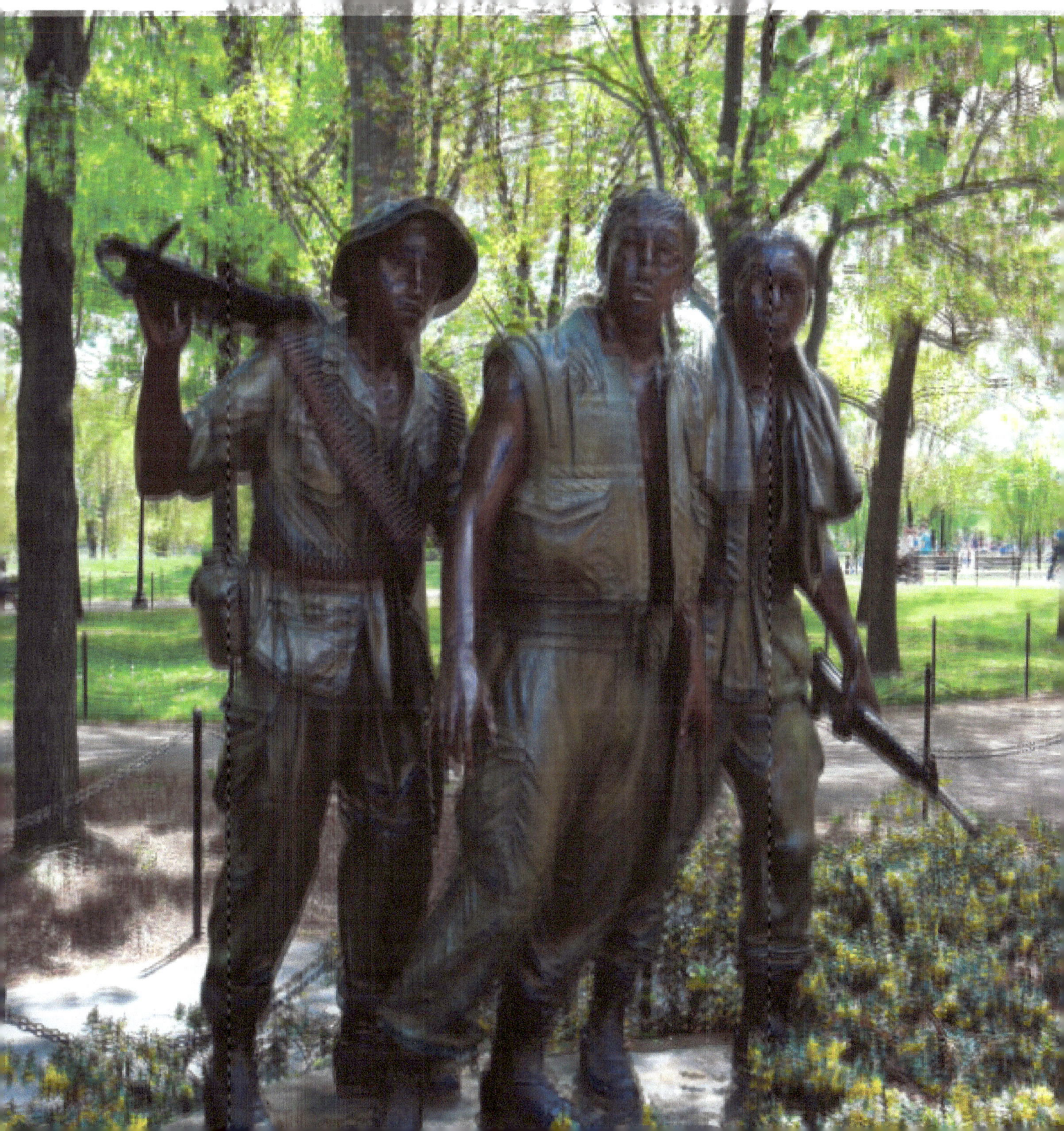

Vietnam was a noble cause imperfectly pursued

~ Ronald Reagan

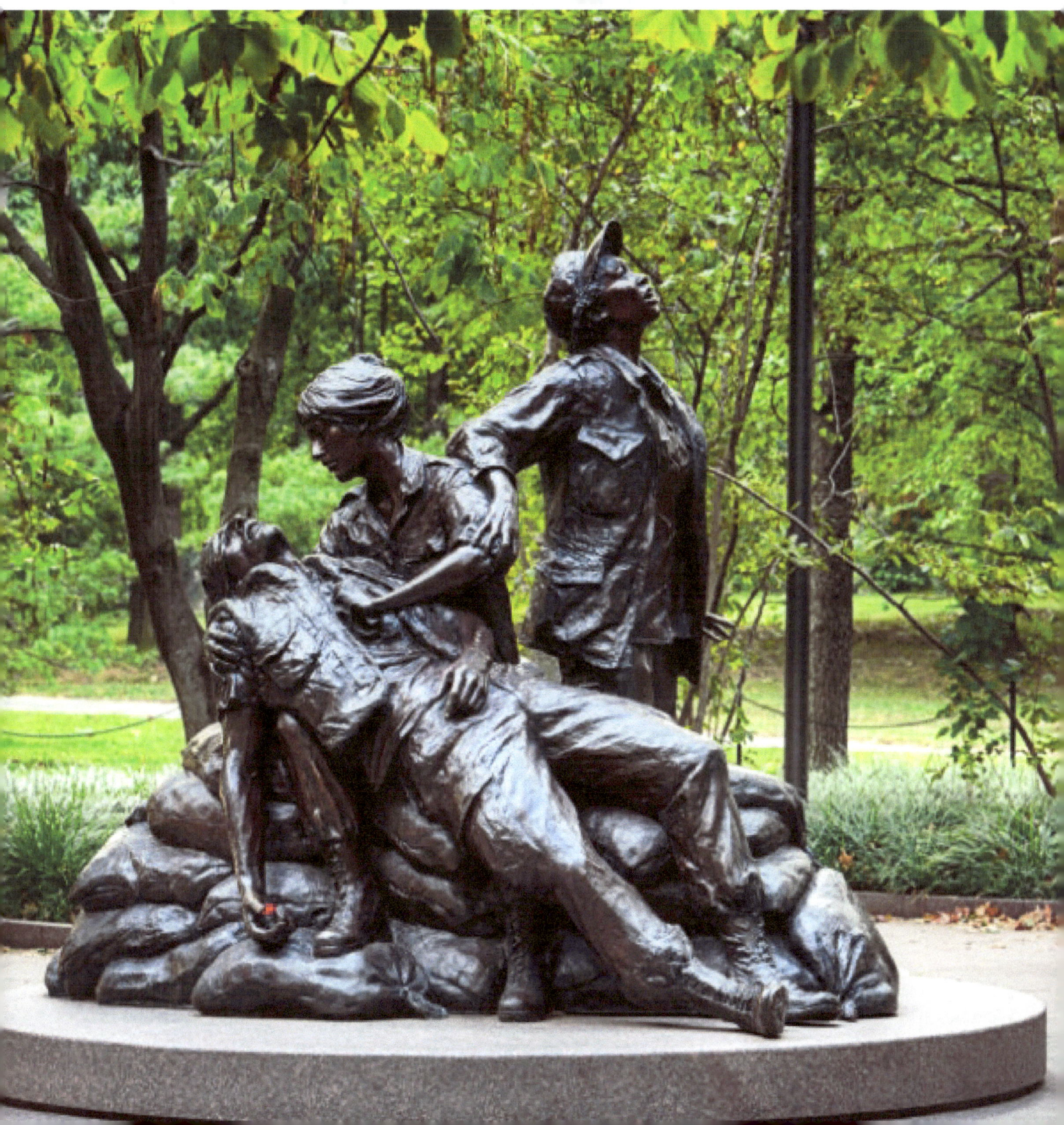

Safety and security are the most basic job of government. I understand that – both as a mayor who works every day to secure public safety and reduce crime, and also as someone who deployed in uniform to Afghanistan because I believed joining the military was part of my duty to help keep my country safe.

≈ Pete Buttigieg

AFGHANISTAN
2001

There is never a bad time to show kindness and provide hope.

~ B. T. Robb

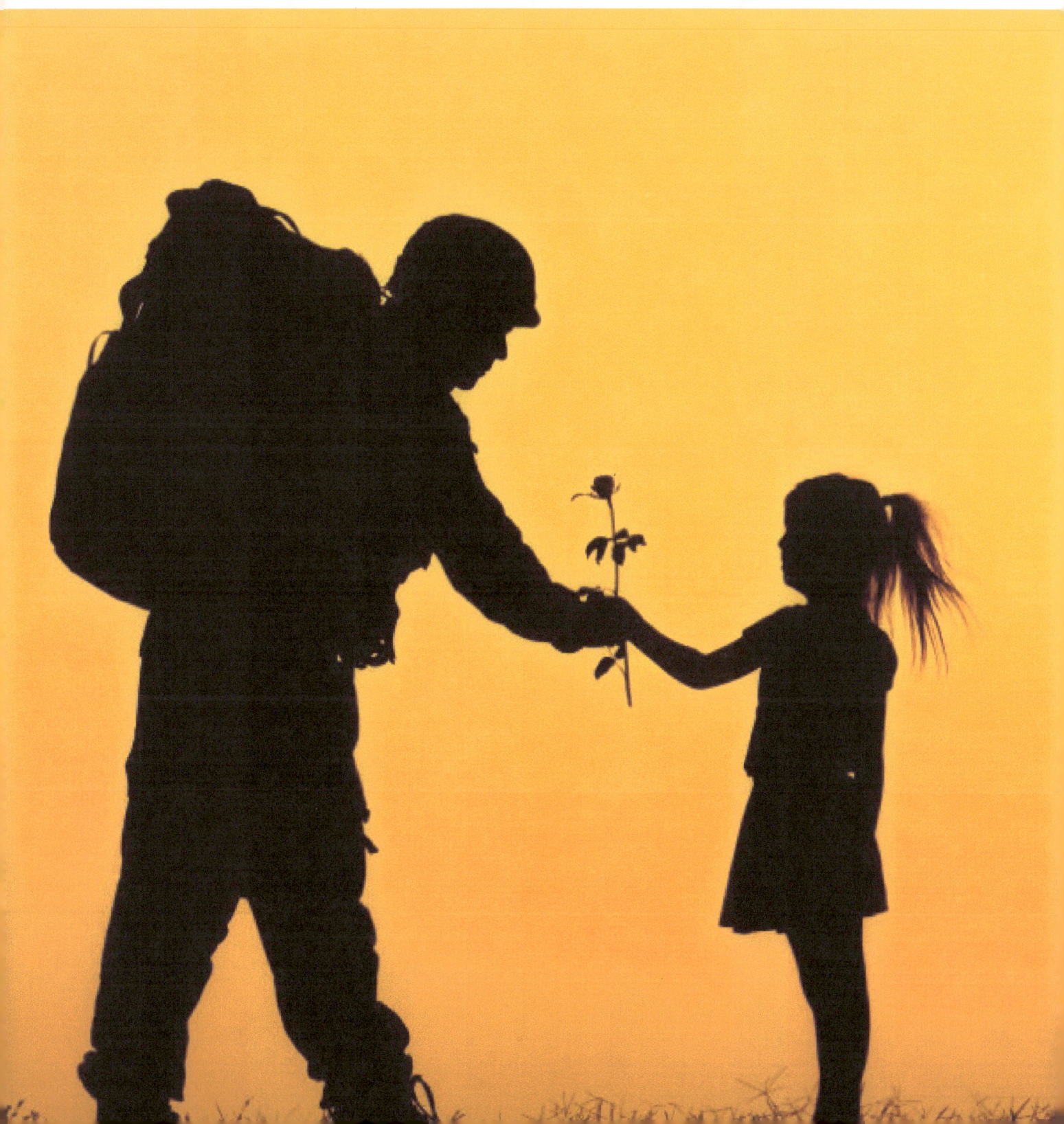

I'm glad you asked. It has nothing to do with oil, literally nothing to do with oil.

≈ Donald Rumsfeld

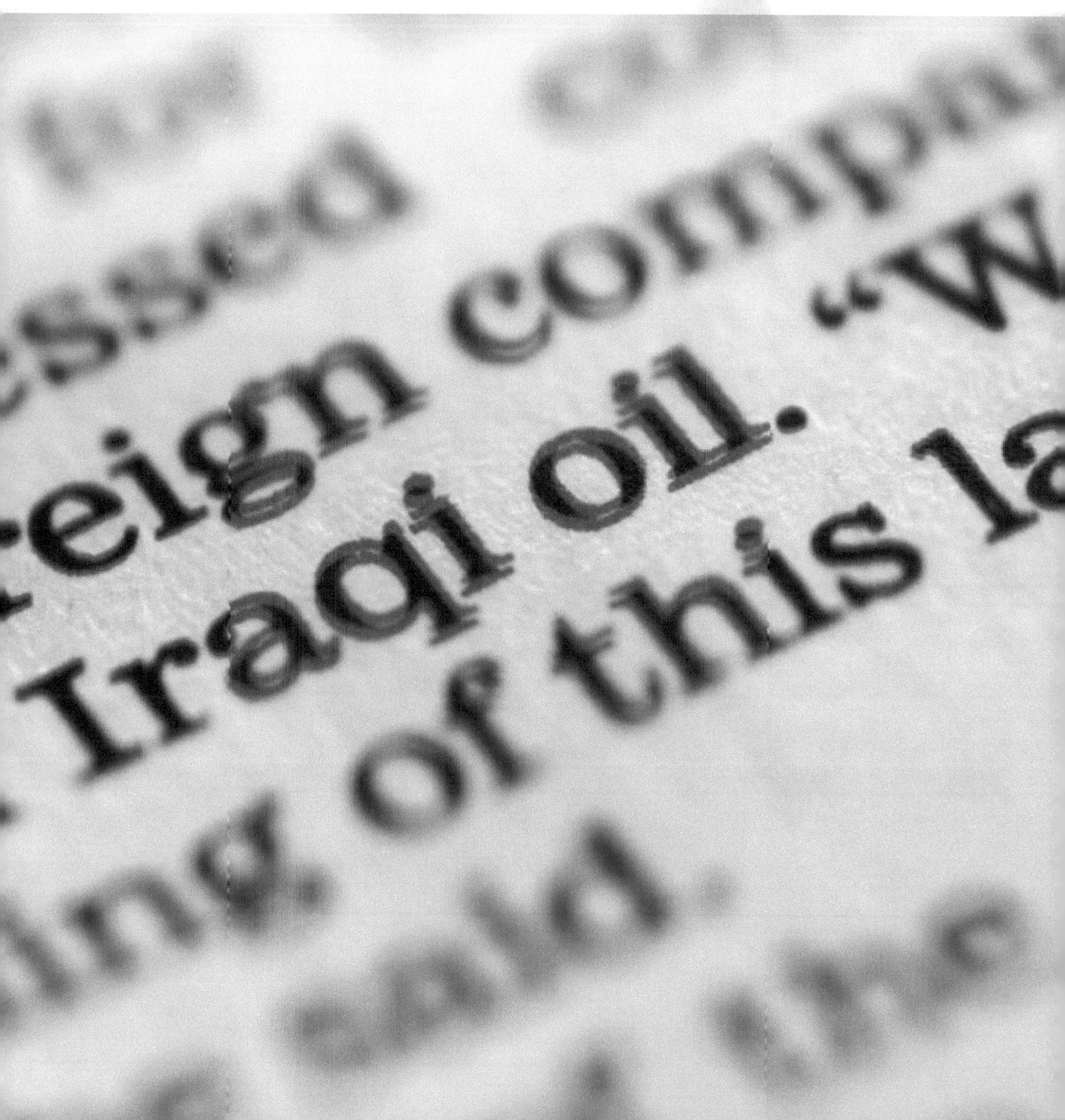

There are some who feel like — that the conditions are such that they can attack us there. My answer is, bring 'em on! We've got the force necessary ...

~ *President George Bush*

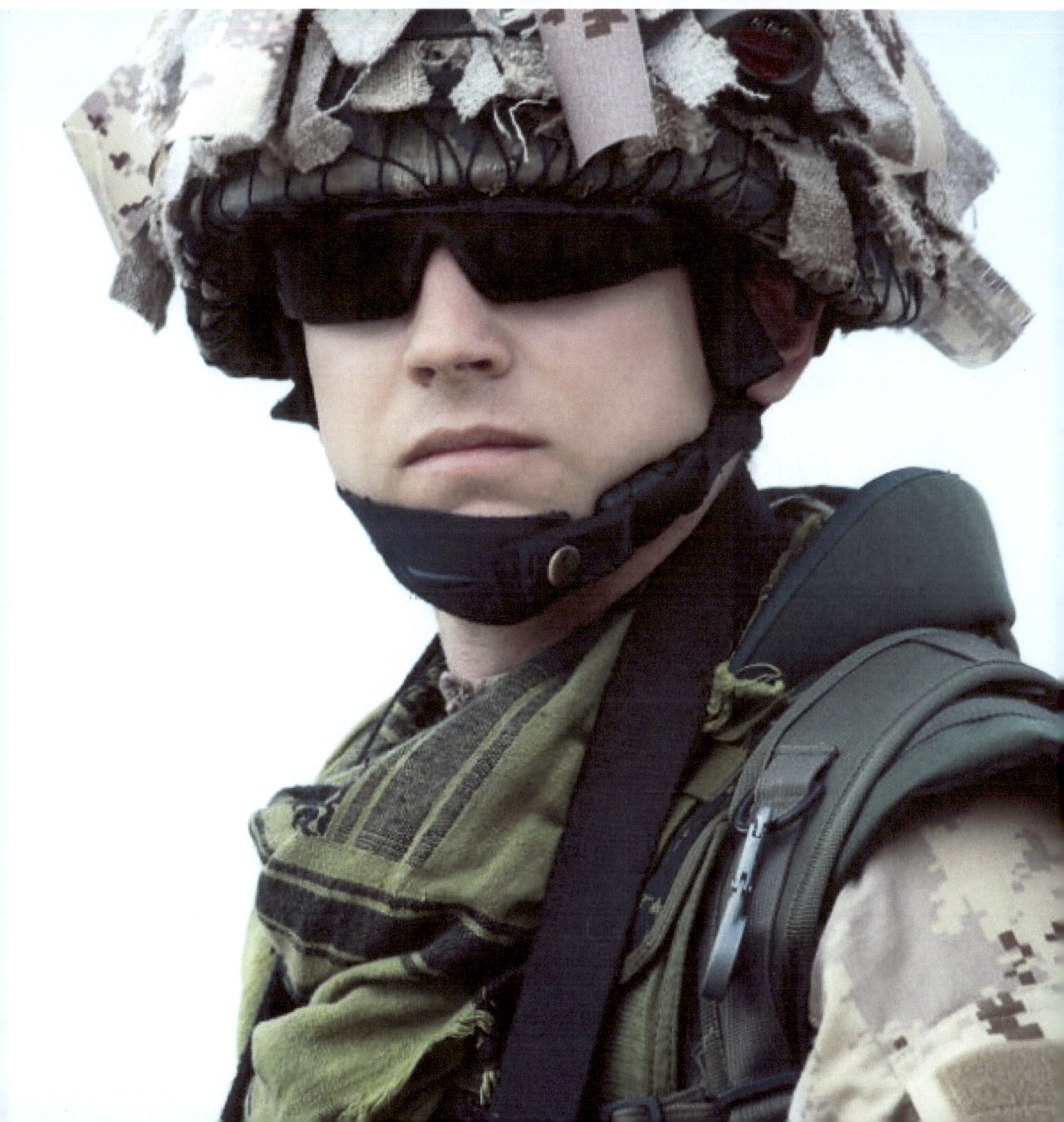

For all of the warriors that have come home to their families: Thank you for your service and a job well done. For those that made the ultimate sacrifice for their country: May God bless your souls and provide peace and comfort to your loved ones.

≈ B. T. Robb

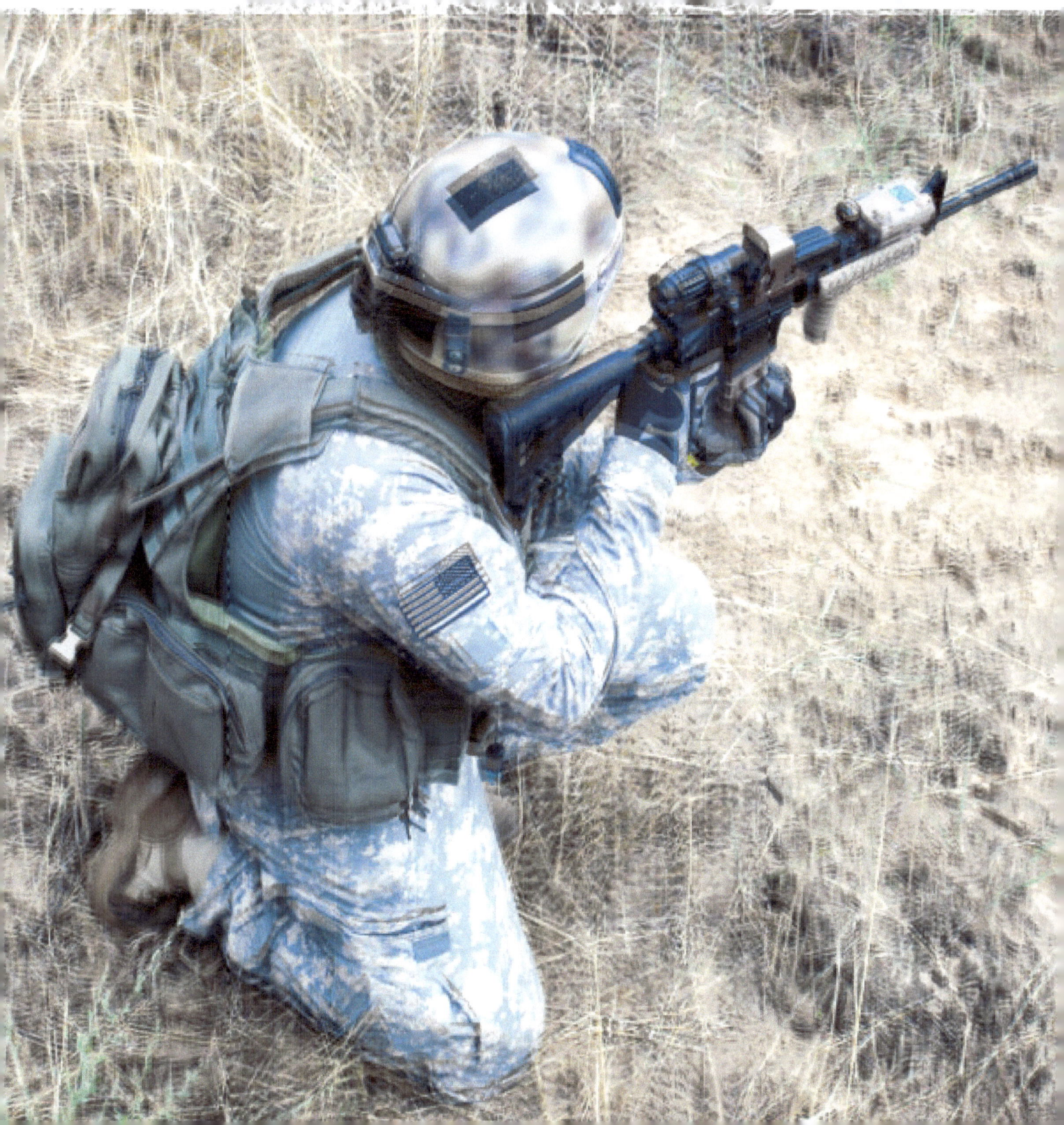

www.ingramcontent.com/pod-product-compliance
Lightning Source LLC
Chambersburg PA
CBHW051934210526
45473CB00006B/2242